From the edge of
the deep green sea

Till Heike

BookLeaf
Publishing

India | USA | UK

Presentation by *BookLeaf Publishing*

Web: www.bookleafpub.com

E-mail: info@bookleafpub.com

ISBN: 9789358319088

First edition 2023

DEDICATION

For my daughters Claudia and Michael, whom we miss everyday.

1.

Can I trust my own heart
to sit in sadness
as it would in happiness
Honestly, I run from them both
Failing in misery and busy
to feel the gifts of both
Accept the change
to be grateful
I am still here
In my one life
This one time we have
With these lessons
Found while drowning
allowing me to love deeper
then I have ever before
The joy and pain are killing me.
Maybe we just hurt so deeply
we crave the light as relief

2.

I have never seen a dead body
I mean a dead body first hand
up close
Even at 5 years old when my great grandmother
died
They wouldn't let me see her body
So now here I am
the first dead body I will see
and hold
will be my own daughters
But first I have to birth her

3.

in August we hold hands
lotion by our side
eyes adjusting
innocence
we gather the dreams
once thought
never mine
above my bed
another day
and raise my head
to meet it
flow of life
song of hope
feel new days riding home
I bow my head to June
she shows all her memories
wiping juice from the chin
of May
years pass
we love
parts die
parts live
riding horses into the deep
barefoot in the sand

4.

you are a collection of lyrics
from all the songs I wrote
when I didn't know you

a leaf sits beside me
not freshly fallen green
these are red and tan
and curling
contorting
in all the wrong places
yellow in the centre
like an old bruise
from a football game
I poke it with my finger
and hold it down against the cement
with one finger, i drag it
hearing it the scrap
and scratch in protest
I swipe it back and forth
a quick little song
dead, but still pleasurable
it has one last melody to share
as I hold it in my hand
an impulse I cannot control
I listen to the sound of
all its veins collapsing
within the palm of my hand

6.

6

The moon in the sky at Midday
I still wonder
I still dream

7.

Songbird
lull me to sleep
because in my dreams
I am complete

the high price of love
rejoice your presence
the weight of devestation
fills your absence

Songbird
lull me to sleep
for in my dreams
We are complete

8.

I birthed a death
she has no breath to live
her little hand has taken its piece of me
and it's peace from me
this moment births us both
we are joined in our separate
and forever tangled rebirths
I birthed a death
life meets death
hers and mine
mine shivering in fear
hers cooling as death does
her little hand is perfect
as it rest lifeless on my chest
a chest that is waiting
for her a scream so
they can spill over with her milk
my milk comes to nurture
her lips never to reach
gone we are
both leaving our lives
in the quiet of this room

9

i must sit
in the heavy rains of March
her sound
never to leave me

10.

little drop
little beat
hidden deep
safely sleep

little drop
imagine you
and me
and you
warm arms
warm heart
waiting arms
new lights
brighten hearts

little drop
little beat
hidden deep
safely sleep

imagine you
in waiting arms
tears of loss
beats
disarmed

little drop
little beat
safely sleep
forever never
our waiting arms
little beat
silently sleep

11

12

field notes in pen and ink:
I gave her a name I loved
yet will never get to call it out to her

12.

grief is the heavy part of love
grief is the part we wish we didn't have to
experience
grief shows us a depth of love we never knew
existed
to love when gone
I wish I never had to experience the grief of
losing you
but then would mean I would never have
experienced the love I hold for you
that love I still hold strongly
When you are not here to hold tightly in my
arms
my loving arms
a parents arms
left wanting
an embrace that should be
safe and secure
and yet you slipped through
when I would have done anything to save you
given my life for yours
now I know true Grief
it is cold and heavy and silent
on the journey out of the depths of grief
in the things around me I see

bringing that love to coexist
with my loss
side by side my love grew as my
grieving stayed
they are forever connected now
just as you and I are
forever connected
forever together
forever my baby
loved beyond all my expectations
my grief is forever
with your absence
and now and forever
my love is yours

13.

15

resting hearts
we hold hands
the time we had to walk together
hands
forever gently resting
on laps
alone

14.

after the fire burns
it's path through you
I will sit with you as the ashes smoulder
small red lines catch the eyes
as there time luminescence fire up then burn out
the tall proud oak tree
striped of its grace and beauty
char lines run from the base to
last remaining brittle branches
like arms extending to the
unforgiving sky
embers still flicking like fireworks
of a grief now
embedded in the foundations
I will sit with you
tend to your fragile and weary state
I will sit with you
and watch as you grow anew

15.

Ashoks cloud follows me
happy on my way, they care
even when its sunny out
I know my cloud is there
they're raining down all over my world
bringing tears to my eyes
I cry like a thunderstorms
and howl like the wind
when sometimes I am sad
my cloud echo's my hurt in the sky
bright blue and big and bold the sky
they shine onto my face
like a silent lullaby
smiling, I look up for them
my cloud I like close by
pitter patter on my face
their tears fill my eyes
Ashoks cloud
helps me think
that they are like the air around me
and like my breath within me
and even tho I cannot hold them
they are forever in my sky

16.

18

my heart
is made
from
the thin gold line
that shines
through
the crack
in the kitchen
window
at my
grandmothers home

17.

depression
is a lesion
beating at me
relentless
rising from me
relentless
till it is a death
in its hunt
and it hunts
and I am the prey
and I am
the predator
red eyes
focused on my own
red dead heart
ficking my lips
devoured
self destruct
take my fill
of my own soul
never satisfied
until destroyed

18.

sweetheart
let our hearts rest together
so we can begin
all that is
in front of us

19.

21

when all of you has fallen away
what do you choose to pick up

20.

I take my grief to bed with me
each night when as
I kiss my children goodnight
wishing them a night filled with dreams of
happiness
I have one kiss less than I need to
fill my own heart
each day i keep going
and I'm still running to catch up

21

these feelings fit the experience
and they are written all over me
maybe in time they words will fade to nice sun
softened aloofness
but today I wear them like the deep and
irreversible razor wounds they are
they are unpleasant to witness
but they are unbearable to own

www.ingramcontent.com/pod-product-compliance
Lightning Source LLC
LaVergne TN
LVHW050300200726
843509LV00015B/3083